The Impact of NAFTA on U.S. Labor Markets

The Impact of NAFTA on U.S. Labor Markets

Justino De La Cruz and David Riker [1]

U.S. International Trade Commission, Office of Economics

June 3, 2014

Abstract

This paper investigates the effects of NAFTA preferences on labor market outcomes in the United States. First, we review prior literature that has quantified these economic effects over the last twenty years. Then we turn from the past to the present. We ask how NAFTA preference margins affect U.S. labor markets today. We use a CGE model and detailed data on NAFTA preference margins to estimate these economic effects.

1.   Introduction

Debate prior to the passage of the North American Free Trade Agreement (NAFTA) often focused on claims that the trade liberalization would have significant effects on U.S. labor markets, including the dire warning that NAFTA would result in a "giant sucking sound" as millions of U.S. jobs were lost to competition from Mexican workers.

The opposing view was that NAFTA would result in efficiency gains from the expansion of bilateral trade in goods and services but would have little effect on U.S. labor markets. This view was supported by computable general equilibrium (CGE) model-based analyses of the agreement like Brown, Deardorff and Stern (1992). This study used a CGE model with monopolistic competition to predict the economic effects of NAFTA reductions in tariff and non-tariff barriers on the economies of the three countries. The model predicted a 0.2 percent

[1] This working paper is the result of ongoing professional research of ITC Staff and is solely meant to represent the opinions and professional research of the authors. It is not meant to represent in any way the views of the U.S. International Trade Commission or any of its individual Commissioners. We thank William Powers for helpful comments on this research. Please address any correspondence to David.Riker@usitc.gov.

increase in real wages in the United States and changes in sector-level employment that ranged from a 11.6 percent reduction in the U.S. glass products sector to a 0.7 percent increase in the U.S. textiles sectors. The reason for these small magnitudes is straightforward: U.S. imports from Mexico were small relative to the entire U.S. market, and the tariffs on these imports were not large even before NAFTA.[2] Tariffs on Mexican imports from the United States were larger, but the Mexican market was relatively small.

We now have a twenty-year record of trade and labor market outcomes to test these very diverse predictions about the economic effects of NAFTA. There is a large econometric literature that has quantified the impact that NAFTA has had on U.S. employment and wages in retrospect.[3] The general consensus in the literature is that NAFTA has not had significant effects on aggregate labor market outcomes in the United States. More recent contributions to the literature have emphasized exceptions to this rule: they find significant effects on U.S. labor market outcomes, but these effects are limited to certain industries and locations within the United States. In the next section, we discuss this literature.

In the following section, we turn to a different question aimed at the present, rather than past, effects of NAFTA. We document the decline in the share of NAFTA imports in total U.S. imports from Mexico over the years and the recent decline in NAFTA preference margins. Then we estimate the effect of recent NAFTA tariff preferences on U.S. labor market outcomes.[4] We incorporate the data on NAFTA tariff preference margins into a GTAP-based CGE model and simulate how real wages and manufacturing employment in the United States would be different

---

[2] The United States had granted General System of Preferences (GSP) benefits to Mexico prior to NAFTA, as discussed in McDaniel and Agama (2002) and Hufbauer and Schott (2004).

[3] It still remains a challenge to isolate the effects of NAFTA from the many other factors that shifted bilateral trade flows since 1994. Krueger (2000), Hufbauer and Schott (2004), O'Leary, Eberts and Pittelko (2012) and others discuss these empirical challenges.

[4] We are not aware of other economic analyses that address this question, so we hope to make an original contribution.

absent the recent NAFTA preference margins on U.S. manufacturing imports from Mexico. Our simulation does not model the effects of NAFTA reductions in the tariffs faced by U.S. exports and so, by design, it is focusing on aspects of NAFTA that are most likely to have a negative impact on U.S. labor demand and the wages of U.S. workers. Even so, we estimate that recent NAFTA preference margins have a positive effect on U.S. real wages, albeit quite small.

To preview our results, the model indicates that the preference margins have small positive effects on the real wages (and therefore purchasing power) of skilled workers in the United States. The preference margins increase their real wages by 0.008 percent. They have an even smaller positive effect on the real wages of unskilled workers in the United States. The preference margins increase their real wages by 0.003 percent. The effects on manufacturing employment in the United States are also small. The greatest positive employment effects are in the non-ferrous metal products, iron and steel, and machinery sectors. The greatest negative employment effects are in the sugar and apparel sectors. We conclude with suggestions for further research.

2. Econometric Evidence of the Historical Impact of NAFTA on U.S. Labor Markets

The general consensus in the econometric literature is that NAFTA has had fairly large effects on the trade flows between Mexico and the United States but has had little or no effect on aggregate labor market outcomes in the United States.

Mary Burfisher, Sherman Robinson and Karen Thierfelder provide an overview of the early empirical literature on the effects of NAFTA in a 2001 article titled "The Impact of NAFTA on the United States." In their review of the literature, they find little evidence that

NAFTA affected aggregate employment in the three countries. They find that the effects in U.S. labor markets are overwhelmed by other macroeconomic trends in the data.

Willem Thorbecke and Christian Eigen-Zucchi survey the evidence on the labor market effects of NAFTA in a 2002 article titled "Did NAFTA Cause a 'Giant Sucking Sound?' " They conclude that NAFTA has resulted in a dramatic expansion of bilateral trade and has brought some stability to the Mexican economy but that the employment effects have been small. The authors point out that foreign direct investment flows have actually favored U.S. workers over Mexican workers. They attribute the lack of labor market effects to relative size (U.S. imports from Mexico amounted to approximately one-half of one percent of U.S. GDP) and to the low tariff rates in place prior to NAFTA.

On the other hand, some economic researchers adopt a different analytical approach and conclude the opposite. One prominent example is a 2006 briefing paper titled "Revisiting NAFTA: Still Not Working for North America's Workers." Authors Robert Scott, Carlos Salas and Bruce Campbell conclude that rising U.S. trade deficits with the NAFTA countries have led to significant job displacement and declining job quality within the United States. Their estimates are based on calculations of the numbers and types of workers associated with the products that the United States trades with its NAFTA partners. These calculations of job displacement are not specifically tied to the magnitude of the NAFTA tariff reductions. They are based instead on the magnitude of the bilateral trade imbalances since NAFTA entered into force. These imbalances can reflect other macroeconomic factors like exchange rates. The authors estimate that the U.S. trade deficits with Mexico and Canada between 1993 and 2004 displaced production that supported approximately one million U.S. jobs, and that this translated into lower average wages as workers moved into lower paying sectors of the economy.

More recent contributions to the literature have not overturned the consensus of little or no effects of NAFTA on aggregate labor market outcomes in the United States, but they have emphasized exceptions to this general rule: they find significant effects on labor outcomes that are concentrated in certain parts of the country and in certain industries.

John McLaren and Shushanik Hakobyan examine how NAFTA affected wages in local labor markets in the United States in their 2010 working paper titled "Looking for Local Labor Market Effects of NAFTA." The paper is an econometric analysis of the effects of NAFTA reductions in U.S. tariffs on imports from Mexico, and ultimately on the wages of U.S. workers within the United States. The authors use worker-level data from the U.S. Census in 1990 and 2000 to estimate each industry's vulnerability to Mexican imports and the share of each location's employment in vulnerable industries. To measure local vulnerability, they calculate an average of the tariff reductions weighted by local employment in each industry and measures of Mexican revealed comparative advantage in the industry. They distinguish the effects of tariff reductions that already occurred by 2000 from tariff reductions that were anticipated after 2000. The authors acknowledge the consensus view that the overall impact on U.S. labor markets is very small or zero, but they find evidence of economic impacts on specific industries and locations. They find local effects that reflect the spillover onto labor demand in non-traded services workers in the same location as the most vulnerable manufacturing industries. They estimate that the most NAFTA-vulnerable locations were in Georgia, North Carolina, South Carolina, and Indiana, and that a high-school dropout in one of the most NAFTA-vulnerable locations experienced an eight percentage point reduction in wage growth between 1990 and 2000 as a result of the NAFTA tariff reductions. They find even larger industry effects. They estimate that the most protected industries – including footwear, textiles, and plastics –

experienced a sixteen percentage point reduction in wage growth as a result of the tariff reductions.

In a 2011 article titled "Trade Liberalization, Unemployment, and Adjustment: Evidence from NAFTA Using State Level Data," John Francis and Yuqing Zheng estimate an econometric model of supply and demand in the U.S. labor market and examine the effects of NAFTA on unemployment in each state for the period 1977-2007. They take a regional approach that recognizes the differences in post-NAFTA trends across states. Their model allows for the lagged effects of the tariff reductions on unemployment growth. They estimate that NAFTA reduced annual unemployment growth by 4.4 percentage points. They conclude that there was an immediate effect of NAFTA in 1994 but that the impact on U.S. labor markets continued for at least seven years.

David Autor, David Dorn, and Gordon Hanson estimate the effect of import competition on local U.S. labor market outcomes in a 2013 article titled "The China Syndrome: Local Labor Market Effects of Import Competition in the United States." Overall, they find that rising imports, most notably from China, have resulted in higher unemployment, lower labor force participation, and lower wages in the United States. The article specifically addresses the effects of imports from Mexico on U.S. manufacturing employment: they find some evidence of a labor market impact of imports from Mexico, but they cannot separate the Mexico trade effects from the China trade effects.

The recent literature has also emphasized the importance of intermediate goods and inter-sectoral linkages in production. In a 2012 working paper titled "Estimates of the Trade and Welfare Effects of NAFTA," Lorenzo Caliendo and Fernando Parro use a Ricardian model of trade with inter-sectoral linkages to estimate the economic effects of the tariff rate reductions among the NAFTA countries between 1993 and 2005. They estimate sector-level trade elasticities and then use these elasticities to calculate the real wage effects of the NAFTA tariff reduction. They conclude that tariff reductions on imports from the NAFTA countries increased real wages in the United States by 0.17 percent.

3. Estimates of the Impact on U.S. Labor Markets Today

In this section, we address a different question: how do the fully phased-in NAFTA preferences affect wages and employment in the United States *today*? We estimate these effects using a simulation analysis that "removes" the NAFTA preferences by increasing the tariff rates on U.S. NAFTA imports from Mexico to MFN rates.[5] NAFTA revocation is not a serious policy option, but this counterfactual analysis is still useful as a way of quantifying the ongoing impact of NAFTA on U.S. labor markets.

The simulation analysis focuses on tariff preferences on U.S. imports of manufactures, even though NAFTA reduces tariffs on other products and there are many non-tariff provisions in NAFTA that can affect labor demand in the United States, such as the provisions for the national treatment of investment.[6] We calculate the tariff preference margins at the level of HTS eight-digit products. The preference margin is the percentage difference between the rate that would apply if the goods entered the United States without any preferences and the NAFTA rate (usually zero).[7] NAFTA tariff preferences do not automatically apply to U.S. imports from Mexico. To qualify for preferential tariff rates under NAFTA, U.S. importers must claim and document that the shipments meet the rules of origin in the agreement. In our calculations, we take account of incomplete preference utilization by using the tariff rates on NAFTA imports of each eight-digit product rather than an average tariff rate on all imports of the product from Mexico, which would combine the rates on NAFTA and non-NAFTA imports from Mexico.

---

[5] Caliendo and Parro (2012) also report a NAFTA-reversing simulation, though it reverses the decline in average tariff rates from the NAFTA countries between 1993 and 2005 rather than eliminating the NAFTA preference margin as it stands today. They estimate that increasing tariff rates from 2005 rates to 1993 rates would decrease real wages in the United States by 0.3 percent.

[6] Thorbecke and Eigen-Zucchi (2002) discusses several of the non-tariff provisions of the agreement.

[7] The former is calculated as a trade-weighted average of the U.S. imports of the same HTS eight-digit product from Argentina, Brazil, Chile, China, India, Russia, and South Africa that did not claim any tariff preferences.

Table 1 reports the weighted average preference margin on U.S. imports of manufactures from Mexico in 1996 (two years after NAFTA entered into force), in 2004 (ten years after), and in 2013 (nineteen years after).[8] The average preference margin first rose and then fell. It has changed over time for several reasons. First, NAFTA tariff reductions were phased in over the first fifteen years of the agreement, and this increased the average preference margin over time. Second, there has been a rise in the share of imports from Mexico that entered the United States outside of the NAFTA program. This reduced the average preference margin, since non-NAFTA imports from Mexico do not have NAFTA preference margins. Third, there has been erosion in the average preference margin due to the reductions in tariff rates on non-NAFTA imports. Finally, there have been shifts in the product mix of U.S. imports from Mexico. The products have different preference margins, so these shifts account for some of the changes in the average margin.

Recent preference margins are generally lower than the magnitude of the historical decline in tariff rates. This is illustrated in Figure 1, which reports the evolution over time of the tariff rate on U.S. imports from Mexico of certain radios for motor vehicles, a tariff-line product that we have chosen as an illustration.[9] The non-preferential tariff rate was 6.7 percent when NAFTA entered into force in 1994. By 2013, the tariff rate on non-NAFTA imports of the product from Mexico was 4.4 percent, while the NAFTA rate was zero. In this example, the historical decline was 6.7 percent (from 6.7 percent to zero), while the recent gap between the preferential rate and the non-preferential rate is only 4.4 percent. There are also many products for which the NAFTA and non-NAFTA tariff rates have both been reduced to zero. For these products, the preference margin is zero regardless of the magnitude of pre-NAFTA tariff rates.

---

[8] The weights are based on the customs value of imports at the level of eight-digit HTS codes.
[9] Specifically, the product is HTS code 85272980.

Our simulations use a 2011 baseline from pre-release version 9 of the GTAP database. We focus on the preference margins on U.S. imports from Mexico in the 21 manufacturing sectors in the database. We do not model the effect of NAFTA reductions in the tariffs on U.S. exports.[10] In this regard, we follow McLaren and Hakobyan (2010).[11]

Table 2 reports the contributions of the NAFTA preference margins to the real and relative wages of skilled and unskilled workers in the United States. The preferences increase the real wages, and therefore purchasing power, of skilled workers in the United States by 0.008 percent. This is the difference between the percentage decrease in the price of skilled labor and the percentage decrease in the consumer price index. Consumer prices fall by more than the price of skilled labor, so real wages increase. The preferences also increase the real wages of unskilled workers in the United States, but only by 0.003 percent. They increase the skill premium in U.S. wages by 0.005 percent.

The real wage effects are smaller than estimates in the literature that we have reviewed, including the 0.2 percent increase in U.S. real wages in Brown, Deardorff and Stern (1992) and the 0.17 percent increase in U.S. real wages in Caliendo and Parro (2012). This is not surprising, since our estimates include the potentially negative shocks to U.S. labor demand (the reductions in tariffs on U.S. imports from relatively labor-abundant Mexico) but do not include many of the likely positive shocks to U.S. labor demand (the reductions in tariffs on U.S. exports to Mexico and Canada). It this sense, our estimates could be viewed as a lower bound on the positive effects of NAFTA on aggregate real wages in the United States. Also, as we have emphasized above, we are simulating the effects of recent NAFTA preference margins, which can be much

---

[10] We discuss the possibility of adding these preference margins in the next section.

[11] McLaren and Hakobyan (2010) also focus on the tariff reductions on U.S. imports from Mexico. However, unlike their study, we estimate the effects on average wages in the United States, while they estimate the effects on wages in especially "vulnerable" locations within the country. Also, they model monetary wages, rather than real wages, so their model does not include the benefits of reduced consumer prices.

smaller than the historical tariff reductions that are used in the models in Brown, Deardorff and Stern (1992) and Caliendo and Parro (2012)

Table 4 reports the impact of the preferences on employment in each of the manufacturing sectors. The model assumes that the total labor force is fixed, so there are no net employment changes in the U.S. economy. However, there is a reallocation of employment among the different sectors of the economy. Some of the sectors decline as the preference margins increase import competition; other sectors grow even though they also experience an increase in import competition due to the preferences, because labor is reallocated away from the contracting sectors. The model estimates that the greatest positive effects on manufacturing employment are in the non-ferrous metal, iron and steel, and machinery sectors (0.4, 0.2, and 0.2 percent increases, respectively), while the largest negative employment effects are in the sugar and apparel sectors (0.7 and 0.3 percent declines, respectively).

4.   Ideas for Further Research

In this section, we sketch a few ideas for extending this line of research. First, our estimation of the effects of current NAFTA preference margins has relied on a CGE model that assumes an integrated national labor market in the United States. Following the recent emphasis in the econometric literature, it would be interesting to try to estimate the effects on local, segmented labor markets within the United States, though this would require a different modeling framework.

Second, we would like to add the NAFTA preference margins on Mexican imports from the United States. We expect that adding Mexican preference margins into the model will increase the simulated positive effects on real wages in the United States.

Finally, we would like to go beyond our analysis of tariffs and try to model the labor market effects of the non-tariff provisions of the agreement.

References

Autor, D., D. Dorn and G. Hanson (2013): "The China Syndrome: Local Labor Market Effects of Import Competition in the United States." *American Economic Review* 103(6): 2121-2168.

Brown, D.K., A.V. Deardorff and R.M. Stern (1992): "A North American Free Trade Agreement: Analytical Issues and a Computational Assessment." *The World Economy* 15(1): 11-30.

Burfisher, M.E., S. Robinson and K. Thierfelder (2001): "The Impact of NAFTA on the United States." *Journal of Economic Perspectives* 15(1): 125-144.

Caliendo, L. and F. Parro (2012): "Estimates of the Trade and Welfare Effects of NAFTA." NBER Working Paper 18508.

Francis, J. and Y. Zheng (2011): "Trade Liberalization, Unemployment and Adjustment: Evidence for NAFTA Using State Level Data." *Applied Economics*.

Hufbauer, G.C. and J.J. Schott (2004): *NAFTA Revisited: Achievements and Challenges*. Institute for International Economics.

Krueger, A.O. (2000): "NAFTA's Effects: A Preliminary Assessment." *The World Economy* 23(6): 761-775.

McDaniel, C.A. and L.A. Agama (2003): "The NAFTA Preference and US-Mexico Trade: Aggregate Level Analysis." *The World Economy*.

McLaren, J. and S. Hakobyan (2010): "Looking for Local Labor Market Effects of NAFTA." NBER working paper 16535.

O'Leary, C.J., R.W. Eberts and B.M. Pittelko (2012): "Effects of NAFTA on U.S. Employment and Policy Responses." *OECD Trade Policy Working Papers*, No. 131.

Scott, R.E., C. Salas, and B. Campbell (2006): "Revisiting NAFTA: Still Not Working for North America's Workers." *EPI Briefing Paper*, No. 173.

Thorbecke, W. and C. Eigen-Zucchi (2002): "Did NAFTA Cause a 'Giant Sucking Sound'?" *Journal of Labor Research*.

Table 1:

NAFTA Share of Imports and Preference Margins over Time

	1996	2004	2013
Average Preference Margin on All Imports from Mexico	3.4413%	3.6253%	1.7440%
Non-NAFTA Share of Imports from Mexico	23.92%	40.51%	42.42%
Average Preference Margin on NAFTA Imports from Mexico	4.5231%	6.0940%	3.0288%

Table 2:

Simulated Effects of the NAFTA Preferences on U.S. Workers

Impact on Real Wage of U.S. Workers	Percentage Point Increase
Skilled Workers in the U.S.	0.008
Unskilled Workers in the U.S.	0.003

Impact on Skill Premium	Percentage Point Increase
	0.005

Table 3:

Simulated Effect of the NAFTA Preferences on U.S. Manufacturing Employment

Percentage Point Increase in the Sector's Employment

GTAP Sector	Skilled Workers	Unskilled Workers
Textiles	0.104	0.112
Apparel	-0.308	-0.305
Leather	0.048	0.054
Lumber	0.074	0.081
Paper and Printing	0.035	0.041
Petroleum and Coal Products	0.008	0.014
Chemicals, Rubber, and Plastic	0.073	0.079
Non-Metallic Mineral Products	-0.044	-0.038
Iron and Steel	0.183	0.192
Non-ferrous Metal Products	0.359	0.370
Fabricated Metal Products	0.022	0.028
Electronic Products	-0.013	-0.007
Other Machinery	0.187	0.195
Motor Vehicles	0.006	0.012
Other Transportation Equipment	0.106	0.114
Other Manufactures	0.097	0.104
Vegetable Oil	-0.007	-0.002
Dairy Products	0.045	0.050
Sugar Products	-0.735	-0.736
Other Food Products	-0.035	-0.030
Beverages and Tobacco	0.045	0.050

Figure 1

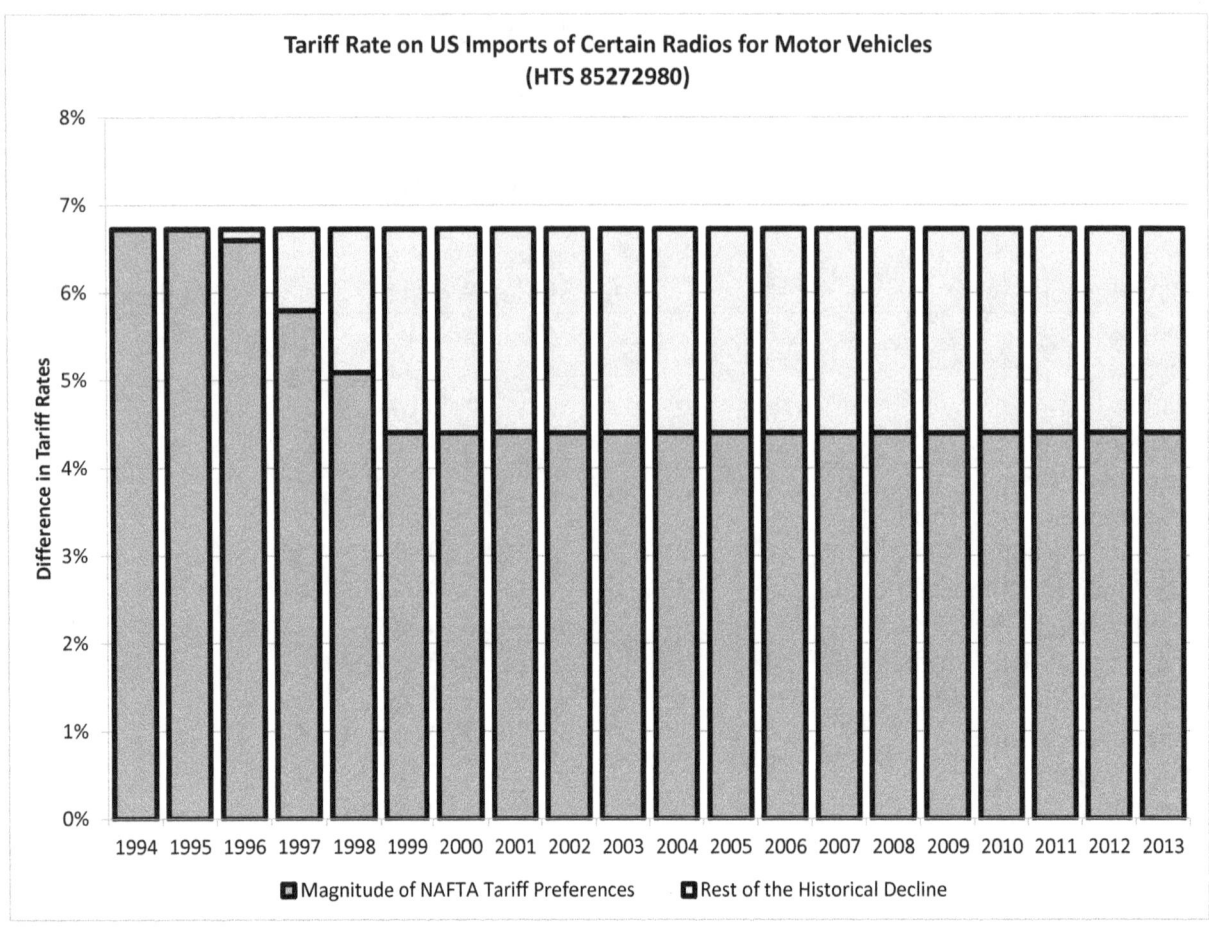